ST. JOHN
THE DIVINE, ARVA

Faith in Community for 200 Years!

St. John the Divine, Arva
Copyright © 2022

All rights reserved. No part of this publication may be reproduced, distributed, or transmitted in any form or by any means, including photocopying, recording, or other electronic or mechanical methods, without the prior written permission of the author, except in the case of brief quotations embodied in critical reviews and certain other non-commercial uses permitted by copyright law.

Tellwell Talent
www.tellwell.ca

ISBN
978-0-2288-4913-1 (Hardcover)
978-0-2288-4912-4 (Paperback)

TABLE OF CONTENTS

Introductory Letter from the Bicentennial Committee v
In the Beginning: From Ireland to Arva 1
The Settlers Come to Canada 4
William Geary's Life in England 6
William Geary's Life in Ireland 8
William Geary's Life in Canada 10
A Short History of the Anglican Church of St. John the Divine, Arva 13
St. John the Divine, Arva: A Short History 14
Addendum: 1951-1997 25
Reaching Out 30
The Ministries of St. John the Divine 1997-2021 34
Friendship Group 37
Sunday School 39
Other Gatherings at St. John the Divine 41
Outreach Committee 42

INTRODUCTORY LETTER FROM THE BICENTENNIAL COMMITTEE

In 2015, a committee was formed with a mandate to raise funds and plan and stage events surrounding the approaching and much anticipated Two Hundredth Anniversary of the founding of the congregation of St. John the Divine, Arva. It was determined that planning would be done in three stages – fundraising, event planning and event staging.

Fundraising activities included the organization of Community Concerts (2), Ladies Gently Used Clothing Sales (2), Holy Smoke Community BBQs (2), Soup and a Bun, Spaghetti Dinner and a Harvest Supper. The events were enthusiastically endorsed and supported by Church Council, which generously allocated 20 percent of general church fundraising events from 2015 until 2021. In excess of $10,000 was raised toward the support of bicentennial year events.

To assist Committee initiatives, long-term parishioner and artist Joanna Gooder donated an ink sketch of the church, which was digitized and used to make the official stationery. Additionally, a St. John's insignia was designed and applied to some Committee communications as well as to the church website.

The congregation was surveyed for ideas to enhance bicentennial celebrations, and the of event ideas were listed and submitted to Committee to determine suitability, practicality and crowd appeal.

Separate sub-committees were formed to develop and purchase promotional materials, to plan each fundraising event and to organize anniversary celebrations.

Despite the interruption of bicentennial planning by the Covid-19 pandemic, the activities that were staged by the Bicentennial Committee were enjoyed by everyone and served to pull the congregation together, to some extent helping to involve the local community and increase the profile of the celebratory year.

IN THE BEGINNING
FROM IRELAND TO ARVA

BY: ALICE LINDEN

"In 1818, when the first people to settle as a group in London Township came out from Ireland with Captain Richard Talbot, there was no church waiting to receive them, and for the first four years their religious life was shrouded in mist. Then, on a summer's day in the year 1822... we see the beginnings of the Parish of St. John's, Arva."

Thus begins the tantalizing glimpse of our parish's origins described in handwritten notes prepared for an address by academic Eleanor Jared, widow of St. John's long-time rector, Rev. Arthur Jared, and found among Dr. Jared's papers following her death in 1973.

We can only guess at the loneliness, uncertainty and unending backbreaking work that filled the lives of these settlers during their first years clustered around the Proof Line as it passed Concession 7 at the tiny settlement of St. John's.

But we want to know more. Who were these courageous souls? Why did they leave Ireland? How did they make their way to Canada West as this part of Ontario was known then? What skills did they bring with them?

Records show that a scattering of individuals had settled in the area in the first years of the nineteenth century, but the first organized settlement began in 1817 with a letter from Captain Richard Talbot of Tipperary (described by F.T. Rosser in his book *London Township Pioneers* as "a gentleman of means") to Earl Bathurst, secretary of state for the colonies.

Talbot had lost heavily during the economic upheaval following the Napoleonic Wars. Prospects looked grim and Talbot had a young family. He decided to sell his property, convert all his assets into cash and emigrate to Upper Canada. Hence his letter to Earl Bathurst, December 29, 1817, appealing for government assistance to emigrate to Canada.

The Earl's reply came in a circular letter noting that the government had ceased to encourage individuals to emigrate alone but would assign large grants of land to persons agreeing to take out and locate at least ten settlers, each of whom would receive a 100-acre grant. There was a catch: the sponsor must first deposit 10 pounds for each settler he proposed to take out. The deposit would be repaid to the sponsor after the settlers were located. The government would provide free transportation, but the settlers would have to pay for the cost of victualling (on a journey sure to take many weeks).

Rosser tells us that Mr. Talbot was willing to accept these terms, and quickly canvassed his neighbours asking who would wish to accompany him to Canada under his leadership. The response was so great that in only six weeks Mr. Talbot wrote again to Earl Bathurst on February 7, 1818, asking about payment of his deposit and stating that he would soon make formal application for at least thirty settlers. These – together with their families – would total one hundred individuals or more.

In fact, the number of applicants was soon so great that Talbot could not handle it. To hold the deposit, for which he was responsible, at a manageable level, he kept the number of "settlers" to a minimum and cleverly equalized the size of families by a brilliant "redistribution" of their children and by classifying young people as "apprentices" and "servants."

On March 7, 1818, exactly a month to the day after having written to the Earl to inquire about payment of his deposit and informing him that he would soon make formal application for at least thirty settlers – who with their families would bring the number of individuals to about one hundred or more – Talbot wrote again to the Earl. Despite having received no reply to his letter of February 7, Talbot was now ready to proceed: This time he dispatched his application – and enclosed a list of his settlers. These numbered exactly thirty but with their dependants totalled two hundred and twenty-one! Not yet finished, the same afternoon he dispatched a second letter, adding the names of two more settlers and their families for a total of sixteen more people.

The application was now for thirty-two settlers and two hundred thirty-seven people, an average of 7.4 persons per settler! A twenty-first century reader could only wish to have been present as the Earl absorbed this information.

Mr. Talbot was not finished. He carefully explained to Earl Bathurst that he was very anxious to make an early start in order to reach Canada in time to put in a crop that could mature early enough to provide sustenance during the winter, and asked for a ship to be sent to an Irish port as early as possible in April – the next month!

Mr. Talbot sent the required deposit, 320 pounds, to the Colonial Office, but Earl Bathurst informed him that the government did not intend to pay for the transport of more than four members per family.

Note

St. John's Bicentennial Committee is grateful for assistance received from a variety of sources, including Diocese of Huron Archives, as it gathers information about those involved in our parish's beginning and St. John's long history. The preceding account of Richard Talbot's extraordinary leadership is based largely on information contained in *London Township Pioneers* by Frederick T. Rosser (1975); *A Short History of the Anglican Church of St. John the Divine, Arva,* an account by Eleanor C. Jared; historical books on London Township provided by Masonville branch London Public Library.

THE SETTLERS COME TO CANADA

Richard Talbot's lengthy correspondence with Earl Bathurst, secretary of state for the colonies, concerning Talbot's application to lead a group of Irish immigrants to Canada occupied much of the early part of 1818.

When word arrived that a ship would pick them up in Cork, members of the party sold their property in Tipperary, bade farewell to friends and travelled to Cork – to find no ship there ready to take them aboard.

By now the group included ninety-one males and ninety-two females. Quickly their food and money began to run out, and there was mounting concern about arriving in Canada in time to gather enough food for the first winter. After waiting five days, Talbot again wrote to Bathurst. Three times. He received no reply.

The brig *Brunswick* finally arrived June 8. After having spent six weeks waiting in Cork, the group finally set sail June 13. So diminished were the settlers' resources that the government agent in Ireland and Talbot pleaded for supplies to be issued to them on their arrival in Canada.

In his book *London Township Pioneers*, from which these excerpts are borrowed, historian Frederick T. Rosser describes the thirty-three-day crossing of the Atlantic as "trying." Most painful among the heartbreaks endured must have been the loss of so many children: "Twelve buried at sea and as many more on islands between Newfoundland and Quebec."

At Montreal, delay occurred again while there was a search for Durham boats to carry new arrivals into the interior, heading for the "Upper Province." A twenty-first century traveller used to being whisked by air between continents can sympathize with those new arrivals – a considerable portion of the original group – who, for reasons of exhaustion or depleted finances, opted to strike out on their own, at least temporarily, at various locations in the "Lower Province."

The journey from Lachine to York turned out to be the most challenging state, according to Rosser, taking three weeks. In York, though, perseverance was about to be rewarded! Richard Talbot happened to meet a distant cousin, Colonel Thomas Talbot, who recommended that the new arrivals settle in London Township. Richard Talbot trusted the colonel's judgement, and on September 11 the group set out for Port Talbot on the north shore of Lake Erie. Even then, reversal awaited: On Lake Erie, the ship they were aboard was wrecked, and they were stranded in the United States.

Soon the group was back in Canada, appropriately at Port Talbot. Good to his word, Colonel Talbot assigned to the weary arrivals from Tipperary land in London Township.

Arrangements were made for the women and children to stay at settlers' homes in Westminster while the men, with Canadian help, went to the lots and erected cabins. The Richard Talbots moved into theirs December 2, 1818, while some other families located next spring. Each of the emigrant families must have had their own adventures. Next is the story of one of those families.

WILLIAM GEARY'S LIFE IN ENGLAND

BY: RAY JONES

On July 28, 1822, nearly 250 people arrived at the Gearys' barn on the 6th Concession (Sunningdale Road) in London Township for the first Anglican Service to be held under the auspices of St. John the Divine. Twenty children were baptized that day by the Reverend Charles James Stewart, who had been invited by William Geary's wife Elizabeth. Construction of a wooden church began in 1823 on land donated by the Fraleigh family at the corner of Richmond Street and Medway Road.

Here is the story of the family that hosted St. John's very first service in their barn in 1822.

William Geary was one of seven children (three boys and four girls) born to William Geary and his wife, Ann, nee Freeman, in Ringstead, Northamptonshire on February 9, 1780. William senior (1747-1800) and his wife, Ann, (1750-1820) were married in nearby Denford on April 10, 1769.

With the Napoleonic War between England and France (1803 to 1815) only a few years away, England was preparing for war. In 1777, William Senior was named Constable of the Ringstead Militia, a group of thirty-three local men aged 18 to 45 charged with "defending the Realm." It was similar to the Home Guard in England during WW II. In 1796, four years before his death, he was promoted to Chief Constable of a group of several militias.

William Senior owned a 73-acre arable farm, which was advertised for sale on May 2, 1801, eight months after his death, by his son William. At 2020 prices, the farm would have been worth approximately 750,000 English pounds.

After William Senior's death, his wife Ann at some point moved back to Denford where she died in 1820, age 70. In the absence of a will, it is assumed that the proceeds of the sale of the farm went primarily to support widowed Ann for the remainder of her life. William Geary Junior at some point made his way to Tipperary, Ireland, where he is found in 1805 renting a farm at the time of *his* marriage to Elizabeth Jones.

The untimely death of his father, William Senior, in 1800, the sale of the family farm in 1801 and the threat of war with France may have contributed to William's decision to move to Tipperary.

A few interesting details about Ringstead

In 1801 when William left, Ringstead had a population of 450 people. Today Ringstead has a population of 1,500 people.

In subsequent years, William's nephew William was left equipment and 10 pounds, and William's niece Jane was left 10 pounds, both by the Reverend Isaac Gaskarth who had officiated at William Geary Junior's baptism. In 1817, nephew William was a churchwarden at St, Mary's in Ringstead.

Ringstead's St. Mary's Church of England was built ca. 1240. It was built of local ironstone as are many of the older houses in the town of Ringstead. In 2007, four local churches, Including St. Mary's Ringstead, formed the "Four Spires Benefice" to improve liaison and communication between the four churches.

WILLIAM GEARY'S LIFE IN IRELAND

William Geary's Uncle, Robert Evans, who immigrated to Ontario thirty years after William did, infers that when William arrived in Ireland he went "inland to introduce...the iron plough [new to Ireland] and he made Professional visits...and hunted and drank with the Irish Gentry." However, at the time of his marriage to Elizabeth Jones he was a farmer on a rented farm in the north of County Tipperary close to King's County, which is present day County Offaly.

The marriage took place November 26, 1805, in Gaelic, at Templeharry Church – the "Church of the Rock" – at the junction of southern County King's and northern County Tipperary. William was 25 and his wife, Elizabeth, age 30. The marriage was officiated by the Reverend John Jones of the Church of Ireland, father of the bride.

Elizabeth's parents, John Jones and his wife, Letitia, had four children, two boys and two girls. John died in 1830 at the approximate age of 80, and Letitia died in Dublin in 1850, age 95.

William and Elizabeth Geary had five children:

- John baptized in County Tipperary in 1808,
- Sarah baptized in County Tipperary in 1810,
- Ann baptized in County Clare in 1812,
- William Jones baptized in County Clare in 1813, and
- Eliza baptized in County Clare in 1814.

These dates suggest that the family continued to farm in County Tipperary until approximately 1811, at which time they moved to County Clare so that William could be appointed General Manager for the estates owned by Bindon Scott in County Clare. Newspaper accounts during the early nineteenth century make several references to disputes in Court between Bindon Scott and his tenants. No doubt William Geary would have been involved in resolving these disputes during his seven-year tenure with Bindon Scott from 1811 to 1818 approximately.

William and Elizabeth Geary and their family emigrated with Richard Talbot's group in 1818. To give a picture of what the times were like, author Donald MacKay in his book *Flight from Famine* quotes Edward Talbot, the son of the applicant Richard Talbot: "Thousands of unfortunate sons and daughters of Ireland were at this time contemplating removal to North America. I became an exile, not as a matter of choice, but of necessity, not with a view of realizing a fortune in the transatlantic wilderness, but of escaping penury and its consequent miseries in the land of my nativity."

And to give a picture of what the emigrants stood to lose, MacKay goes on to describe what the applicant's background was: "Richard Talbot, forty six, a militia officer and squire of Cloughjordan, had enjoyed a comfortable living as had his ancestors who had moved from England 200 years earlier with Cromwell. Now like many of his kind, he was caught between falling income and rising prices. The end of wartime prosperity convinced him that there was no future for his family, or indeed for Ireland, and he sought government aid to emigrate to Upper Canada, where his brother, John, had settled."

The group sailed from Cork aboard the 550-tonne brig *Brunswick* on June 13, 1818. There were four cabins on board the ship and the Geary family occupied one of them. Newfoundland was sighted thirty-one days later on July 14, and the ship anchored off Quebec City on July 29. The passengers were transferred to the steamer *Telegraph* for the trip to Montreal.

WILLIAM GEARY'S LIFE IN CANADA

The ship's passengers arrived in Montreal on August 5 and then Prescott on September 1. A number of passengers decided at this point to put down roots in the Ottawa Valley, leaving the rest of the passengers to transfer to the *Caledonia* on September 3. This vessel arrived in York (Toronto) on September 9, Niagara on September 11 and then on the way to Port Stanley they ran aground at Dunkirk, New York, on September 25.

On September 25, the small American schooner *Humming Bird* made three trips to Port Stanley carrying a total of fifty passengers. At this point the group had been in transit from Cork, Ireland, for approximately fifteen weeks, of which only four and a half weeks were at sea.

On arrival in Middlesex County, William Geary was allocated the north half of Lot 14, Concession 5, southeast of the present location of St. John the Divine Church in Arva. When he left Ireland, he had 300 British pounds. In Middlesex County, he was allocated 300 acres of which he quickly cleared 30 acres, and he had one yoke of oxen, six cows and eight calves. William's son John, age 17, was allocated the south half of Lot 14, also 300 acres. The soil conditions were considered exceptionally good. The first home William Geary built for his family in Middlesex County was called Wilton Cottage.

The Geary family was involved in the building and running of the settlement. In 1824, William Geary was appointed Roadmaster for Concession 3, and in 1826 he was elected Clerk of the Township. He was re-elected in 1834 and 1839. Since William and his son John had been given deeds to their properties, they had the right to vote.

In 1833, the brothers John and William Jones Geary, ages 25 and 18 respectively, were given a contract to build log houses in the Townships of

Adelaide and Warwick for $15 each. They continued to perform similar work, building log cabins for early immigrants to Adelaide Township, logging for the Canada Company and building bridges and roads. They also built two schooners that sailed Lake Ontario: the *Elizabeth* and the *John and William Geary*.

John Geary (1808-1873), the eldest Geary offspring, married Eliza Haskett (1814-1889) in 1833 and they had eight children.

- First son, George, (1835-1911) married Ellen Harding in 1864. He built and operated a grist- and saw-mill on the Thames River known as Plover Mills. Later he became an oil refiner and invested in Imperial Oil and, with brother John, imported Aberdeen Angus cattle from Scotland.
- Second son, William, was a druggist who moved to the United States, was married in San Francisco and later moved to Sacramento.
- Third son, John Jr., (1839-1928) married Mary Smart (1832-1895) and became a lawyer with partner George Moncrieff. He became a founding partner of Imperial Oil in 1880 and built the Geary Cheese Factory, which operated until 1901.
- The first daughter, Mary Jane, (1841-1930) married Justus Ingersoll, whose parents founded St. Mary's in 1841.
- Fourth son, Theo, (1843-1881) married Mary Goodson in 1871. He had a drugstore in Strathroy before relocating to Sarnia.
- Second daughter, Elizabeth ("Bessie"), (1845-1931) married James Sutherland, a merchant of Maxwell in Grey County. After his death, she married Anglican clergyman Rev. Richard Dixon.
- Fifth son, Robert, (1847-1906) was a farmer who married Eleanor Marshall in 1889.
- Sixth son, Richard, (1853-1921) was a druggist who joined his brother Theo in Sarnia. He never married.

Sarah (1810-1894) and her younger sister Eliza (1814-1898), second and fifth children of William and Elizabeth Geary, did not marry and remained at their parents' farm, Wilton Cottage. They later moved to Geary Avenue close to Fanshawe Park Road and Adelaide Street until their death.

Ann Geary (1812-1856), third child of William and Elizabeth Geary, married Samuel Hunt Park who, in 1836, was governor of the London Jail. They were married by Rev. Benjamin Cronyn at St. Paul's Cathedral in 1851. They had one son but unfortunately Ann died in 1856.

William Jones Geary (1813-1855), fourth child of William and Elizabeth Geary, married Elizabeth Rich (1818-1863) in 1841 in Goderich. Their only child, Charles Palmer, was born in 1849 at Wilton Cottage. W. J. Geary was a road contractor, land speculator and horse breeder and at various times lived between London and Goderich.

Notes

Flight from Famine by Donald MacKay

A SHORT HISTORY OF THE ANGLICAN CHURCH OF ST. JOHN THE DIVINE, ARVA

BY ELEANOR C. JARED
WITH AN ADDENDUM 1951-1997
BY MARGARET A. BANKS

Eleanor Croysdale Jared, who died in 1973, was the daughter of Archdeacon W.J. Doherty and Mrs. Doherty and the wife of the Reverend Arthur H. Jared, Rector of St. John the Divine, Arva, from 1950 to 1974. A distinguished scholar, she was a Doctor of Philosophy of Harvard University. Amongst other academic appointments, she was Professor of English at Huron College, London, and was its first Professor Emeritus.

Dr. Jared's history of St. John's was originally given as a talk, probably in the late 1950s. After her death, the text was found in her own handwriting among her papers and was published in 1975 to mark the centenary of the present church building. It was reprinted as St. John's celebrated the 175th anniversary of the 1822 service, which led soon afterwards to the building of the original frame church.

Margaret Amelia Banks, who died in 2010, was a graduate of Bishop's University, Lennoxville, Quebec (BA, 1949), and the University of Toronto (MA, 1950; PhD, 1953). From 1953 to 1961, she was on the staff of the Archives of Ontario. From the latter year until taking early retirement in 1989, she was Law Librarian at the University of Western Ontario where she also held faculty appointments in Law and Graduate History. She is the author of books and articles on topics relating to history, law and parliamentary procedure.

Although Ms. Banks only became a member of St. John's Arva in 1994, she developed an interest in its history. She was grateful for the help of longer-standing members of the parish in preparing the addendum to Eleanor Jared's history.

ST. JOHN THE DIVINE, ARVA: A SHORT HISTORY

BY ELEANOR C. JARED

The Beginning

In 1818, when the first people to settle as a group in London Township came out from Ireland with Captain Richard Talbot, there was no church waiting to receive them, and for the first four years their religious life was shrouded in mist. Then, on a summer's day in the year 1822, the mists clear away, and we see the beginnings of the Parish of St. John's, Arva.

On that 28th of July, so long ago, almost the whole countryside was still empty of human habitation. Grassy glades were interspersed everywhere by stands of hardwood: maple, beech, elm, hickory and Canadian walnut, with here and there a few white or red pines, and, in swampy places, clusters of cedar and tamarack. The Proof Line (now Highway 4, Richmond Street North), surveyed a decade or so earlier by Mahlon Burwell, was simply a narrow track, twisting and winding, while the tree stumps and concession roads were scarcely marked trails. Here and there, however, in small clearings in the woods or on some open plain, could be seen a rough shanty with its rougher log barn nearby.

One such small farm clearing was visible between what are now the Fifth and Sixth Concession roads near Adelaide Street North. This farm belonged to William Geary, who had come with Richard Talbot and other settlers from Tipperary to hew out for themselves homesteads in this brave new world.

Had we been standing in that primitive farmyard on that warm late summer day in 1822 we should have seen men, women, and children approaching it from every direction. Up the Proof Line from the south, down from the north, and along the narrow Fifth Concession trail they came; some on horseback, some in ox carts, and many on foot. One man named Robson, who lived ten miles off northwest on the Seventh Concession, walked doggedly every foot of the way with his wife and family of boys and girls, so desirous were they of being there.

What was it that had drawn these folks from their shanties and cabins far and near in the lonely bushland, some 250 strong, leaving their household tasks, their soap-making and berry-picking and their grain fields ripe for harvest? The answer was a man who came out of the farmhouse and entered the barn wearing the very long white surplice of the early nineteenth century clergyman. William Geary's wife, Elizabeth, herself a rector's daughter, had been instrumental in bringing this clergyman to give to the people of the Talbot Settlement the rites and sacraments of the Church of their fathers.

The clergyman was the Honourable and Reverend Charles James Stewart, son of the seventh Earl of Galloway, namesake of Bonnie Prince Charlie, and Master of Arts of Corpus Christi College, Oxford. He had left all the comforts of civilisation and home in order to bring the comfort of religion to these solitary settlements in the Canadian wilderness as a travelling shepherd of a scattered flock.

After the service, many of the mothers and fathers came forward with their children, babies in their mothers' arms, toddlers holding their fathers' hands, twenty in all, and also three grown-ups, and as they formed a circle around the minister on the trampled mud floor of this primitive barn, he took them each in turn and the solemn words of Baptism hallowed the summer air: "...I baptise thee in the name of the Father, and of the Son, and of the Holy Ghost." Then, comforted, strengthened, and renewed, the people returned home by the ways they had come, back to their forest homes in this strange and lonely land.

Amongst the names of the people baptised by Dr. Stewart on that day[1] are some still familiar on the parish lists of St. John's and in the Township of London:

- Michael & John, children of William & Bridget Colbert
- John, son of Joseph & Catherine Sifton
- John Wright, son of Charles & Esther Sifton
- Nancy, wife of Jacob Freligh

- John, son of Jacob & Nancy Freligh
- Charles, son of John & Elizabeth Freligh

It was Mr. Freligh, as the name is now spelled, who gave to the parish the two acres on which St. John's stands. Among the sponsors, too, are many familiar names such as William & Elizabeth Geary, in whose barn the service was held, and who were the ancestors of Mr. Leigh Farncomb. Others are Thomas Shoebottom, John Ardiel, and Leonard & Rebecca Ardiel, who are of the family of Mrs. Bart Powell. The name Talbot also occurs.

Such were the beginnings of the Mother Church of London Township.

The First Church

It would appear that as a result of Dr. Stewart's visit in 1822 the settlers began to think of building a church. Freeman Talbot, son of Captain Richard Talbot who first brought the group to this country, in a letter to Verschoyle Cronyn, states that a frame church was built in 1823[2]. At that time it was shingled, roughly sided, but not completely finished, having a temporary floor and also very temporary windows.

This building is referred to by the Reverend Alexander Mackintosh who had come to St. Thomas in 1824 and made occasional visits to the parish, baptising the children, taking marriages, holding services, and infrequently administering Holy Communion. In 1827, Mr. Mackintosh had received a questionnaire from Archdeacon (later Bishop) Strachan of Toronto, seeking information from the clergy about the district of which they had charge. In his reply, he stated that he occasionally preached in London in two places (in the village and the township) and that in London (township) there was on the Seventh Concession "a frame church building." This frame church was the first St. John's, Arva[3].

The Early Years

Records of the Ontario Historical Society contain the lists of baptisms, marriages, and burials performed by Mr. Mackintosh from 1824 to 1829, which include those of this parish, and over and again occur the names of Sifton, Shoebottom, Talbot, Powell, Guest, Fitzgerald, Ardiel, O'Neill,

Geary, Scatchard, Orr, Lawrason, Robson, and Colbert, all of them well known today. In 1827, on Thursday, August 2, Dr. Stewart, now Bishop of Quebec, came to London Township again, accompanied by Mr. Mackintosh, and confirmed thirty people, among whom were Sarah and Ann Geary, Margaret Talbot, Maria Sifton, Catherine Sifton, Stephen Powell, Ambrose Powell, Margaret Shoebottom, and Thomas Shoebottom.

Late in 1829, Mr. Mackintosh was sent from St. Thomas to open up the mission of March and Bytown (now Ottawa[4]) and so disappeared from the London Township scene. In the same year, the Reverend Edward Jukes Boswell was transferred from Sandwich to London, so now at last London village and township had a resident clergyman of their own. In 1832, however, after three brief years, Mr. Boswell went to Montreal and London was again without a spiritual director. Shortly thereafter, the Reverend Benjamin Cronyn arrived from Ireland on his way to the settlers in Adelaide Township. He was persuaded, instead, to remain in London, where he took charge of St. Paul's in the village and St. John's in the township.

The story of the rectorship and the episcopate of Benjamin Cronyn, that tremendously important story of the early years of London and the founding of the Diocese of Huron, has been told many times, and *Benjamin Cronyn; First Bishop of Huron* by Dr. A.H. Crowfoot has been published. There is no opportunity in this short account to do justice to this. It should be noted, however, that in 1836 the Parish of St. John's, London Township, and St. Paul's, London Village, were formally constituted as two of the famous Crown Rectories established by the then Lieutenant Governor, Sir John Colborne. Benjamin Cronyn was, of course, the first rector of both parishes.

In 1839, the district of London became part of the new Diocese of Toronto, which had been formed from the western part of the Diocese of Quebec. In September of the following year, Dr. John Strachan, first Bishop of Toronto, made his first visitation to this section of his diocese and officiated in St. John's Church. Of this visit, Dr. Crowfoot in his biography of Benjamin Cronyn records that no less than sixty-four persons "came forward to renew their Baptismal engagement" (Confirmation). "It was truly gratifying," wrote the editor of *The Church*, "to witness a temple so thronged in a spot which, a few years before, had been a wilderness."

After the service, a deputation waited upon the Bishop to tell him how important it was that they should have a rector of their own.

This came about in 1841 when Mr. Cronyn gave up the Parish of St. John's to devote himself to the rapidly growing Parish of London, which had recently been made a separate village. The Reverend Charles C. Brough, later Archdeacon of London, was appointed Rector of St. John's.

During Archdeacon Brough's regime, which lasted until 1872, the frame church was at last completed when, in 1845, Mr. Brough employed John Haskett, a carpenter, to lay the floor and erect a pulpit and pews. Mr. Cronyn, during his term of office, had found time in his busy life to conduct services in houses and barns in the district, which is now the Parish of St. George's, London Township.

Shortly after he became Rector of St. John's, Mr. Brough opened the first St. George's Church on the farm of George Robson on the Thirteen Concession Road. At this time Mr. Brough was also in charge of the whole region to the north as far as Lake Huron, where there was not one resident clergyman or minister of any denomination. However, in 1844 the Reverend Henry C. Cooper was appointed travelling missionary to the Devonshire Settlements in the Townships of Stephen and Usborne. He was succeeded there in 1849 by the Reverend Archibald Lampman, father of the famous Canadian poet. Mr. Lampman looked after the Huron District, St. Mary's and Biddulph Township[5] and thus released the Rector of St. John's. Later, from 1862 to 1864 Archdeacon Brough was assisted at St. John's by the Reverend John Philip DuMoulin, who married one of the Archdeacon's daughters. Mr. DuMoulin later became Bishop of Niagara.

Some items of interest are to be found in the St. John's Vestry Book of Archdeacon Brough's period. In the report of the Vestry meeting at St. John's in 1848 this note occurs: "...it was agreed that no cattle should be allowed to pasture in the churchyard except those belonging to the Sexton[6]."

In 1849, the Church collections amounted to £4.19.8.[7] The Expenses:

- To the Sexton's wife for washing the Rector's surplice: £ 0. 3. 6
- For wine: £ 11.10 ½
- To Sexton: £ 1.16. 1 ½

- For cutting firewood: £ 1. 3
- Total: £ 2.12. 9

In 1853, it was resolved to charge the sum of 10 shillings for the opening of the burial ground to all members of the Church of England who did not contribute to the ministry of St. John's, and for the use of the burial ground for all persons not members of the Church of England the sum of one pound; paupers to be allowed free interment at the direction of the Rector and churchwardens. For opening a grave the Sexton was empowered to charge one dollar, except in the case of children who died under the age of 10 years. For non-members of the Church the fee was two dollars[8].

In the 1840s, the hour for a fashionable wedding was 11 a.m. At that hour on a day in 1858, Ann Sales was married to Bamlet Sifton. Ann's mother bought the silk for her dress in London at $1.50 a yard. Her sister, the bridesmaid, had a more expensive dress at $2.00 a yard.

Their velvet bonnets cost $5.00 each; kid gloves $2.00 a pair. They also wore buttoned shoes of fine kid. The men were dressed in high silk hats and black broadcloth suits with cutaway coats. After the ceremony came the wedding dinner. The tables were laden with roast turkey, roast goose, pies, cakes, cookies, the wedding cake and many other dishes. In the afternoon the young people took out the horses and carriages and went for a drive. At five o'clock in the afternoon they returned for supper. After this the fiddler took his chair in the corner and the dancing was in full swing. At midnight all sat down to another large supper. The dancing went on till three or four the next morning. Sometimes in these early days the wedding guests stayed to breakfast.

For Miss Sales' wedding her mother had bought a large triangular loaf of white sugar for $2.00. This was used for the wedding cake and the punch; usually the family used maple syrup. The tea for the wedding cost 75 cents a pound[9].

It was during Archdeacon Brough's rectorship that the Diocese of Huron was constituted and the first Rector of St. John's, the Reverend Benjamin Cronyn, elected its bishop in 1857. He was the first bishop in Canada to be elected (former bishops had all been appointed by the Crown) and the last to be consecrated in Lambeth Palace Chapel, London,

England. Succeeding bishops in Canada were to be consecrated in their own diocesan cathedral.

The Present Church

On Easter Day, in 1873, the Reverend J. Walker Marsh, Archdeacon of London, entered upon his rectorship of St. John's, succeeding Archdeacon Brough, who had died on March 14 of that year at the age of 79 years. Under Archdeacon Marsh's leadership and guidance, the present brick church of St. John's was built, and consecrated by Bishop Hellmuth on December 12, 1875. The last marriage performed in the old church was that of Tena Smibert and Charles Powell. These were of the family of the late Bart Powell, who had been a prominent and active member of St. John's during his lifetime.

Canon J. B. Richardson, who succeeded Archdeacon Marsh, was inducted as a rector on April 9, 1899, by Bishop Baldwin. Two months later, in June 1899, the Parochial Guild was organised at Lyndhurst, the home of its first president, Mrs. Esther Sifton Thurston. For some reason the meetings later discontinued for a while, but in 1908 the Guild was reorganised. According to its constitution, the Guild was to aid in any work for the good of the church and the parish. Among the names on the membership list at that time are those of some families familiar in the parish today:

- Honorary President: The Rector's wife, Mrs. Richardson
- President: Mrs. Thurston
- 1st Vice-President: Mrs. Cary
- Secretary-Treasurer pro-tem: Mrs. Marshall
- Members: Mrs. Graham, Mrs. Newcombe, Miss Stark, Miss M. Newcombe, Miss Marshall, Miss B. Richardson (later Mrs. Boucher), Miss Campbell, Mrs. George McComb, Miss Priddis, Mrs. Thomas McComb

Soon afterwards, a Chancel Guild was formed, two members taking a month at a time in looking after the Altar and Sanctuary[10].

In 1906, members of St. John's who lived between Huron Street and the Fourth Concession gathered under Archdeacon Richardson to plan a new church which should be closer to their homes than St. John's. Thus was born St. Luke's, Broughdale. The Venerable J. B. Richardson was rector of the parish for over twenty active years. When he retired on June 29, 1919, it was with these words, "Here endeth the record of my church services of twenty years and three months, 'the night is far spent, the day is at hand[11].'"

A beloved Irish rector in the person of the Reverend William Lowe succeeded Archdeacon Richardson, and he was followed in 1925 by another golden-tongued Irishman, the Reverend S. E. McKegney. When the Reverend T. H. Farr was Rector of St. John's from 1928 to 1935, his two sons, Beverley (later to become Rector of St. John's, Sarnia) and Maurice (later to become Rector of St. John's, London), were studying for Holy Orders at Huron College, an honour for the Parish of St. John's.

The Reverend A. Kinder, who succeeded Mr. Farr, was another beloved rector. In 1945, the Reverend T. D. Lindsay became rector for a busy three years while he attended Huron College. He was succeeded by the Reverend J. H. Pogson, who was appointed to the parish in 1948. During his short term of office Mr. Pogson paid particular attention to the missionary work of the church, as did Mrs. Pogson, who also used her splendid talents to further the Christian education of the children of St. John's.

Restoration

In 1950 the Reverend A. H. Jared was appointed Rector of St. John's, and under him the restoration of the fabric of the church was immediately begun. A choir vestry was added, and a new heating system and new organ were installed. The beautiful chancel furniture, a stained-glass window, and other furnishings were the generous gifts of devoted parishioners, and the former Township Hall was renovated to serve as a parish hall.

St. John's, Arva, has also been the mother church for six churches in the Township of London. Its daughter churches are:

- St. George's, London Township established 1841.
- Trinity, Birr, established 1867 under the Reverend William Davis.
- Emmanuel, London Township, established 1882 under the Reverend Robert Fletcher.

- Church of the Hosannahs, Hyde Park, established 1888 under the Reverend Robert Fletcher.
- Grace Church, Ilderton, established 1896 under the Reverend A. H. Rhodes.
- St. Luke's, Broughdale, established 1906 under the Venerable J. B. Richardson.

During almost all the years that London Township has existed, a church dedicated to St. John the Divine has stood on the corner of the Proof Line and the Seventh Concession. It has looked out upon the Medway; it has looked out upon fire when on more than one occasion buildings in its neighbourhood have burned to the ground.

Its windows flickered in the light of the flames that in 1907 were set alight by jubilant villagers when they burned the last toll gates on the Proof Line. They flicker now as trucks and motor cars flash by in the night and the light on the busy corner blinks on and off. The church has heard the lonely hoofbeats of infrequent horses on the mud track outside its doors, the mud track that was Richmond Street in the earliest days. It has heard the rumble of wagon wheels in later years, the incessant roar of the traffic today. Within its walls children have been christened and confirmed, young people married; and in its churchyard, in due course, its people have been laid to rest. It has echoed to prayers for peace in time of war and rejoicings in victory; to the happy psalms of marriage and the solemn requiems for the dead. Its congregations have grown and waned and grown again. And always, Sunday by Sunday, year by year, its people have continued to come to hear the solemn exhortations of the preacher, the beautiful and comforting words of the Book of Common Prayer, and to share in the solemn Sacrament of the Holy Communion.

They no longer have to tramp or ride laboriously mile upon weary mile to hear the Word of God as on the day of that first service so long ago. But still in this year of grace they listen to the same words of peace and in future years congregations yet to come will, by the grace of God, still hear and heed the loving words of Our Lord, "Come unto me all that labour and are heavy laden, and I will refresh you."

So ends the manuscript of Eleanor Jared.

St. John's Cemetery

No account of St. John's would be complete without mention of the ancient burial ground where for almost a century and a half the families of London Township have laid their loved ones to rest. This plot, a part of St. John's churchyard, was given by the Fraleigh family with that of the church, and a memorial stone records the death of Elizabeth Fraleigh in 1832, and of her husband, 1849, as well as the names of five children who died between the ages of 16 and 24 years.

Chapter 7 of *Up the Proof Line*, compiled for Colonel Douglas B. Weldon by Dr. Fred Landon and the Reverend Orlo Miller, contains an excellent account of the history of the burial ground and its service to the community. Of the present St. John's Church it says that "...while plain as to its exterior, is dignified and beautiful within... one of the most pleasing of the little churches within the Diocese of Huron." A fitting tribute on which to end this brief history of the Church and Parish of St. John the Divine, Arva.

Notes

1. Publication of the Ontario Historical Society, Volume IX, 1910. Record of Baptisms, Marriages, etc., by the Reverend Alexander Mackintosh of St. Thomas, 1824-1830.
2. Transactions of London and Middlesex Historical Society, Part III, 1911. Letter by Freeman Talbot quoted by Verschoyle Cronyn.
3. *The John Strachan Letter Book: 1812-1834*, Toronto, Ontario Historical Society, 1946.
4. Thomas R. Millman, *The Life of the Right Reverend, the Honourable Charles James Stewart*, Huron College, London, Ontario, 1953. Page 208 (Alexander Mackintosh).
5. The Venerable J. B. Richardson, "Historical Sketch of the Diocese," in *Jubilee Memorial, 1857-1907: The story of the Church and First Fifty Years of the Diocese of Huron*, London, Ontario, 1907. Pages 22, 23.
6. St. John's Vestry Book.
7. St. John's Vestry Book.

8. St. John's Vestry Book. Different currencies were in use at the time, hence the references to both shillings and dollars.
9. An interview with Mrs. Esther Talbot, published in *The London Free Press*, February 27, 1933.
10. Notes in "The Parish Guild" made available by the Rector, the Reverend A. H. Jared by the Misses Newcombe of the Fifth Concession, London Township.
11. From notes left by the tenth rector, the Reverend J. H. Pogson.

ADDENDUM: 1951-1997

BY MARGARET A. BANKS

Although published in 1975 to mark the centenary of the present church building, Eleanor Jared's excellent account of the history of St. John the Divine, Arva, was compiled and given as a talk some time earlier. It does not bring the history of the parish much beyond 1950, though there are brief references to events later in the fifties. Dr. Jared died in 1973 and her talk was published posthumously. This addendum briefly sketches notable events that took place in the parish from 1951 to 1997, when it celebrated its 175th anniversary as a worshipping community.

The Restoration of the Church Fabric

Eleanor Jared's husband, the Reverend Arthur H. Jared, was Rector of St. John's from 1950 to 1974. Soon after he was appointed rector, as his wife has noted, the restoration of the fabric of the church began. For a short time the church was closed to carry out some of the work; the congregation then worshipped at one of the St. John's daughter churches, Emmanuel, in Ballymote, London Township[1]. On St. Cyprian's Day, Wednesday, 26 September 1951, a service of thanksgiving was held in St. John's to mark its re-opening. The Right Reverend George N. Luxton, Bishop of Huron, performed the rite of re-opening the church and preached the sermon.

But the work of restoration was by no means complete when the church re-opened. Much remained to be done. As noted in the order of service: "There is yet to be added in carved oak, in stained glass, in embroidered fabric and rich memorial, those things that will make of this Church a shrine of great beauty."

Some important additions were made four years after the re-opening. On Sunday, 4 December 1955, a service was held to dedicate the new furnishings of the chancel and sanctuary, all of which were gifts from

Colonel and Mrs. D.B. Weldon. Included were a prayer desk, the pulpit, choir stalls, the sanctuary rail, the clergy stall, Bishop's chair, the reredos, and the altar. All were dedicated by the Right Reverend W.T.T. Hallam, Assistant Bishop of Huron. It was noted in the order of service that these church furnishings were carved oak, that they represented the finest craftsmanship, and that they added a permanent richness to the church fabric.

Other dedications that took place in the years that followed were of a chalice and paten in memory of Colonel George Wilfrid Little, 20 September 1964, a sanctuary lamp in memory of Oliver Roy Moore and Shirley Ilma Moore, 4 July 1965, and the altar flower vases in memory of Norah Elizabeth Newcombe, 11 December 1966.

On 22 July 1975, a centennial thanksgiving service was held to mark the one hundredth anniversary of the present church building. The Right Reverend David B. Ragg, Bishop of Huron, was the celebrant and preacher. He also dedicated a new organ in memory of Eleanor Jared.

The need for restoration and repair is continuous and a Centennial Appeal Fund was established to raise money to carry out needed work. The "Centennial Retrospect" bulletin noted that the external painting was finished in time for the church to look spic and span for June 22 and that the reshingling of the roof had been completed.

The New Parish Hall

The congregation's most ambitious project in this century occurred following the annual vestry meeting of 1976, at which then priest-in-charge Archdeacon J. Royston Beynon asked, "What do we need?" and Robert W. Packer, a long-time member of St. John's and a former superintendent of the Sunday school replied, "A new parish hall."

For many years, the old Township Hall had served as a parish hall. Though the church was grateful to have its use, the Township Hall had two obvious disadvantages. It was on the other side of a busy highway, and because of its height and shape it was difficult to heat and not really suitable for Sunday school classes. Moreover, it was felt that an opportunity should be provided for fellowship after services; a hall adjoining the church would facilitate such gatherings.

Professor Packer's suggestion therefore met with immediate approval. Member Donald McGugan, an architect, undertook to draw up plans. When the future hall's dimensions had been decided, members of St. John's gathered in the churchyard and formed up to join in the ancient act of beating the bounds, standing shoulder to shoulder in a hollow rectangle for the blessing of the soon-to-be-erected building.

Meanwhile, an energetic fundraising campaign was going forward. The entire cost had been raised or pledged by the time of the hall's dedication by Bishop Ragg on 30 April 1978.

Stained-Glass Windows

Several of the stained-glass windows in the Church of St. John the Divine pre-date the years with which this addendum deals. For example, the oldest window in the church is that in memory of Lieutenant Colonel Thomas D. Bourke, who died on 25 February 1875. It appears to have been installed at the time the brick church was built. Added soon afterwards were stained-glass windows in memory of Thomas and Elizabeth Shoebottom, both of whom died in 1876, and Mary Ann Talbot, who died in 1880. Members of both families were among the original settlers of 1818, who built the frame church a few years later. Other windows were installed between 1880 and 1950, but a great many more have been added in the second half of the twentieth century.

On Sunday, 2 October 1955, the St. Augustine of Hippo window was dedicated. Designed by Robert McCausland Limited of Toronto, it portrays St. Augustine, Bishop of Hippo in North Africa, in his cope and mitre. In his hands he holds the quill, the scroll, and the Bishop's staff, indicative of his writings and his high office.

In 1958, the four sanctuary windows were dedicated[2]. Like the St. Augustine of Hippo window, they are the work of Robert McCausland Limited. They depict Christ's agony in the garden, His crucifixion, His resurrection, and the coming of the Holy Spirit. They are memorials to Bishop Stewart of Quebec, who conducted the 1822 service, and to the first three rectors of St. John the Divine: Cronyn, Brough, and Marsh[3].

Rectors and Priests-In-Charge

Eleanor Jared's history gives the names of the Rectors of St. John the Divine up to the appointment of the eleventh rector, her husband, the Reverend Arthur H. Jared. To update the history, the names of rectors and priests-in-charge from 1950 to 1997 are listed below:

- Rev. Arthur H. Jared, Rector, 1950-1974
- Ven. J. Royston Beynon, Priest-in-Charge, 1974-1983
- Rt. Rev. Frank F. Nock, Priest-in-Charge, 1983-1986
- Rev. Tim Rowland, Priest-in-Charge, 1986-1987
- Ven. [now Canon] Morley E. Pinkney, Rector, 1987-1991
- Ven. Robert Dann, Priest-in-Charge, 1991-1992
- Rev. Canon David R. Hartry, Rector, 1992-

175th Anniversary Celebrations

The 175th anniversary celebrations of the Parish of St. John the Divine, Arva, began with a well-attended levée in the parish hall on New Year's Day, 1997. It is planned throughout the year to have special services, guest choirs and speakers, and other events. The highlight will be the service on Sunday, 27 July 1997, commemorating the original service held on 28 July 1822.

Conclusion

In conclusion, it should be emphasized that a church is much more than a building, no matter how beautiful its furnishings and stained-glass windows. This addendum has noted some of the major events in the history of the Church of St. John the Divine, Arva, during the last forty-six years, but it is the day by day and week by week acts of Christian worship, prayer, teaching, fellowship, and good works that keep a church alive and vibrant. The rector and wardens, the organist and choir, the Board of Management, the Sunday school, the Cronyn Guild, the Chancel Guild, St. John's Friendship Circle, and, indeed, all members of the congregation have a role to play in ensuring that this beautiful and historic church continues to fulfil its purpose as a worshipping community of town and country people.

As it celebrates 175 years of service, St. John the Divine approaches a new century and a new millennium confident that, with God's help, it will continue to act in accordance with its mission statement, the words of which appropriately conclude this addendum: "Inspired by the love of God, and led by the power of the Holy Spirit, the Church of St. John the Divine seeks to be a welcoming, caring, accepting community of faith, ministering to the wider community through worship and prayer and by sharing our gifts and love in the service of our Lord and Saviour, Jesus Christ."

Notes

1. Emmanuel Church, founded in 1882, closed in 1975. Its memory lives on in the parish hall of St. John's, Arva, dedicated in 1978, through materials and money derived from the sale of Emmanuel Church.
2. I have been unable to find the exact date of the dedication. The parish records include correspondence dated 1957-1958 regarding the four windows, as well as typescript notes of the order of service for the dedication, but they are undated. No church bulletin containing the order of service has come to light.
3. Windows in memory of Bishop Cronyn and Archdeacon Brough were installed in the brick church at the time it was built. See *Dominion Churchman*, vol. 1, p. 246 (25 May 1876) and vol. 2, p. 18 (10 August 1876). Information on what happened to them has not come to light.

REACHING OUT

BY: ALICE LINDEN

Even as Church of St. John the Divine commemorated its 175th anniversary, parishioners found their attention drawn toward the future. In London Township and city – as all over the world – the approaching millennium, just three years ahead, was discussed with lively curiosity and much uncertainty.

"Social change," on many lips a vague, all-inclusive term, hinted at a variety of possibilities ranging from beneficial to troublesome. There were warnings that new approaches, both attitudinal and technical, would be called for to meet the anticipated needs of large numbers of groups, families and individuals coping with accelerating rates of challenge, fracture and re-configuration.

As the old century slipped away, parishioners – looking back – marvelled at the steadfastness of the generations who had followed in the steps of the worshippers at the Geary barn. What challenges now awaited the pioneers of the new millennium?

In an act of faith, a special committee was set up to begin preparations for the parish's bicentennial, to be achieved – God willing – in 2021.

The retirement in 1999 of Rev. Canon David R. Hartry, rector since 1992, led to one of the most significant developments in St. John's history: the advent of the woman priest.

In January of 2000, Rev. Canon Beverley Wheeler, formerly associate rector at St. Paul's Cathedral, accepted an invitation from the parish selection committee and assumed her responsibilities as the first woman rector of Church of St. John the Divine.

Canon Wheeler's ten-year ministry at St. John's was responsible for several significant innovations. Chief among these involved the altar being moved forward, away from the wall, providing the Officiant with a closer visual connection with the congregation during the celebration of the Eucharist.

The importance attached to St. John's youthful members feeling fully included in worship services was illustrated by the introduction of a child-sized wooden cross. The weekly talk to children and members of the Youth Group clustered around the rector at the chancel steps now concluded with selection of a young (and delighted!) crucifer, who held high the cross while leading the procession to Sunday school.

Following the tradition, the children returned briefly during Communion for a blessing at the altar rail.

Canon Wheeler's suggestion that coffee in the parish hall, previously a once-a-month event after Sunday 11:00 a.m. service, be replaced by a WEEKLY social time, proved highly popular. Members were quick to seize the increased opportunity to share news with old friends – and to invite newcomers to join the conversation.

On her retirement, Canon Wheeler was followed by Rev. Susan Baldwin, interim priest until the induction in 2009 of St. John's current priest, Rev. Wendy Mencel.

The Book of Common Prayer, used at the Sunday eight a.m. service, disappeared from the pews at St. John's when that service was discontinued in response to a declining number of worshippers. The Book of Alternative Services is now followed on all occasions.

The traditional Christmas Eve service has also undergone considerable up-dating in keeping with the times. To meet the needs of worshippers unable to attend a midnight service, the traditional Christmas Eve service now takes place in early evening. An earlier, so-named "family service," has been added in the late afternoon, with numerous parents accepting the rector's novel invitation to bring their small children in pyjamas, ready for bed.

While some activities are for entire families, others engage specific groups. For women, the first Monday afternoon of the month is reserved for the re-defined Friendship Group, dedicated to providing service to church and community as well as providing a social time. The third Sunday sees entire families arriving early for a hearty pre-service breakfast served up by the Brotherhood of Anglican Churchmen (BAC) and the youth of St. John's, with proceeds dedicated to sending parish children to the Huron Diocesan camp. A recently formed circle of knitters has created a colourful assortment of prayer shawls, available to the rector and parishioners to take to individuals suffering illness or mourning a loss.

A ministry program for young people has been established, and after much energetic fundraising, two groups of teens made a pilgrimage to France to participate in an international youth gathering at a monastery in Taize.

A week-long summer day camp for children living in the neighbourhood is a popular outreach project for St. John's Sunday school.

The breaking of bread – in reality simple cookies or veritable feasts – has always occupied an important place in the parish's social life. Some meals offer menus following long tradition (pancakes on Shrove Tuesday, lamb on Maundy Thursday). A much-anticipated "Culture Fest" fills the parish hall with aromas of dishes reminiscent of food traditional in countries around the world, prepared by St. John's cooks.

Of course, St. John's has to make sure everyone knows about these activities. Communication techniques unknown a few years earlier were quick to earn for the new century the title "Age of Social Media." In 2006, the parish launched its own website (stjohnsarva.com). The weekly printed bulletin distributed at the door by official greeters takes as its theme "CONNECT WITH US." The warmth of this invitation and availability of easy ways to connect are obvious in the listing of the church's address (21557 Richmond St. at Medway Rd.), telephone number (519-660-8177), fax number (519-660-0946) and most recent addition, its email address (stjadmin@bellnet.ca).

A large sign board positioned at the side of the four-lane highway passing in front of the church keeps motorists informed of the service times and planned events. In the church office, advent of the computer has become an essential tool in such time-consuming but essential tasks as preparation of bulletins and tracking of expenses.

Through such marvels as Facebook, Twitter and Instagram, the rector is able quickly to reach individual members and share parish news – greatly reducing time spent on necessary communications – and even, on occasion, seek thoughtful consideration in preparation for lay participation in upcoming sermon-related discussions.

Seen through the windows of the parish hall is St. John's old cemetery, in which generations have been laid to rest since the land was given to the new parish by the Fraleigh family in 1823. Faded headstones and other memorials bear witness to the seemingly limitless faith of the early generations, who often bore the loss of multiple family members of tender years. More recent inscriptions reflect lives usually lived longer, in more gentle times.

Today the well-tended cemetery describes itself as "NON-DENOMINATIONAL," welcoming people of all backgrounds – sometimes the descendants of early settlers wishing, after decades lived away from the place of their own origin, finally to rejoin their ancestors.

Once simply a burial ground, the enlarged cemetery today provides for a choice of arrangements. A columbarium reached from the church by a landscaped walk provides the inurnment of cremated remains in individual compartments with name identification, while elsewhere is space reserved for in-ground burial after cremation.

Around the cemetery's perimeter, old pine trees stretch and bend. From the church's bell tower rings out the call to worship, familiar to generations.

THE MINISTRIES OF ST. JOHN THE DIVINE 1997-2021

BY: ALICE LINDEN

The church called the Reverend Canon Beverley Wheeler as the first female rector in the over 175 years as a parish. The year was 2000, and Rev. Wheeler commissioned a nursery to be built, the coffee hour began following the 10:30 a.m. service, and the rectory was sold in order to invest the funds. Angus Sinclair came to lead our music program and Wendy Murray (now Mencel) became our Huron student who started and led a youth group. At this time there were three Eucharists per month and two services of morning prayer. In the year 2001, the "new" hymn book "Common Praise" was put into circulation.

In 2002, the parish established a bursary program for Centennial Public School and Medway High School. Both awards were for academic achievement. In 2018, the Medway award was redesignated to highlight the achievements of a foreign student who, like the early settlers of Arva, has left family and friends behind seeking new opportunities in Canada.

In 2003, the then Bishop Bruce Howe established a partnership with the Anglican Church in South Africa and St. John's was twinned with St. Augustine Parish, Payne. A jazz concert was held to raise funds for South Africa and this relationship continued for many years.

During this year, the kitchen received a makeover to bring it up to code for cooking. The parking lot was paved and guest signs were erected to invite newcomers to St. John's. Many fundraising endeavours ensued to raise much needed money for a new organ. Poor Boy lunches, Christmas Market, garage sales, pie making and so much more helped to ensure that music would continue in the style and tradition in which the parish was accustomed.

In 2004, the Ladies Friendship Group came to a close after twelve years of sharing and caring. However, this was not to be the last we heard of a friendship group.

2005 saw the establishment of "Kids Night Out," an evening of activities for neighbourhood kids, the arrival of our new music director Dr. Sean Kim, and the retirement of Rev. Wheeler. Upon her retirement, the Reverend Susan Baldwin was interim priest for six months before the Reverend Wendy Murray (now known as Mencel) began July 1, 2006.

2006 brought a new organ, which was installed on Palm Sunday, and the revival of the Ladies Friendship Group. Youth nights continued, and outreach began to take off with fundraising for Sleeping Children Around the World, Ronald McDonald House, Council of the North and The Primate's World Relief and Development Fund (PWRDF).

In 2007, the Reverend Earl Leiska was formally re-instated as honorary assistant. Rev. Leiska faithfully served the parish for many years holding Bible Study, BAC Men's Group and men's breakfast and conducting worship services.

Also in 2007, the Ladies Group was resurrected and much needed friendship and fundraising ensued. An account of that group follows.

2007 was also the year that the senior Youth Group decided to plan and attend Taize, France, in four years for their pilgrimage. They were very involved in Crash the Cathedral evenings as well as in helping with parish suppers. The parish recognized that we need to spend time and talent on our youth and two youth groups were formed. Each Sunday the youth would meet and discuss current issues of the day. In addition to this, monthly social gatherings were held and continue to be held for the youth.

In 2008, the Men's Group chose to donate all breakfast funds raised to send children in the parish to Huron Church Camp. Several of our children have enjoyed their formative years at the camp and return bringing many memories to share with the congregation. During this year, the parish had the good fortune of having Mrs. Jean Davies as lay reader. Jean shared many heartfelt sermons, led Bible Study and prayer chain, and assembled a team of devoted people to bring the good news to the residents of two local retirement/nursing homes. A highlight was the Christmas service she brought to the homes, complete with our choir and organist.

In the years 2010-2011, the Reverend Kate Hathaway joined St. John's as honorary assistant and became a dear and valued member of the clergy team. Kate is always known to preach a really good sermon.

In the summer of 2011, the Youth Group made their way to Taize for their pilgrimage. This was a life-changing event for many of the youth who had never been on an airplane or away from home. 2000 youth from around the world were involved the week our children attended and with four worship services per day to attend, there was never a dull moment. Friendships were made with other youth who shared the same passion for Jesus Christ.

In 2012, one of the big highlights was the installation of air conditioning in the sanctuary. We said goodbye to humidity and extreme heat and welcomed summer worship with open arms.

2018 saw our men's breakfast commandeered by our Youth Group. We welcomed our youth leader, Nicole Sader, who meets Sunday mornings with our youth as well as for outside adventures like the 30 Hour Famine. This is the year the outreach committee at St. John's really started to make an impact on the world outside our church walls.

Our website and social media began to evolve albeit not without complications. Currently in 2021 we are on Facebook, Twitter, Instagram and of course our website.

FRIENDSHIP GROUP
BY: HEATHER MILLS

This group became an offshoot of the Anglican Church Women (ACW) at St. John the Divine Church in 2007. The ACW Group, as we had known it, was disbanded, and the Ladies Group made a decision to form this Friendship Group in order to continue on with activities to help in outreach ways and our own church.

We meet the first Monday of a month. Our members can be up to thirty-five strong and at meetings we often have about eighteen in attendance.

A lot of time is spent planning our annual bazaar. The entire group pitches in and works hard at making fine foods, such as our famous mincemeat and meat pies. We also make pickles and preserves, chili, cookies, tarts, loaves and party food items to name a few. Silent auction items, fine quality treasures, jewellery, books and a tasty tea room are all available for our shoppers.

It is impossible to name everyone, but we know how much every woman in our church is important and how much we value each other.

We support various outreach groups including My Sisters' Place, Sleeping Children Around the World, Huron Church Camp, Diocese of the Arctic and our own church St. John the Divine.

Families appreciate our help with funeral receptions. The hall is decorated with white tablecloths, floral arrangements and a wonderful spread of food. We are thankful to the ladies of the church who help with this worthy mission.

The Group also enjoys a tour, a road trip and eating out.

Some adventures have included a tour of Heeman's Garden Centre, the Arva Flour Mill, an alpaca farm in Thorndale, The Museum of Ontario Archaeology in London and BrickYard Antiques in Mount Brydges.

Restaurant Ninety One, The Village Teapot in Ilderton and the hot meal at St Andrew's Church at Chippewas of the Thames First Nation Reserve names just a few of our eating spots. We should admit to eating at every meeting as well.

We have hosted and joined neighbouring churches for World Day of Prayer services the first Friday in March. In 2018, we celebrated The Republic of Suriname at St. John the Divine.

During Covid we are taking a hiatus from most of our activities. However, some are still busy working behind the scenes at their homes. We celebrate those in our group still working to raise money, those working to help those in need and those making phone calls to keep in touch.

We join with others
Each one giving
Building our Faith together

SUNDAY SCHOOL
BY: MURIEL VINCENT

In the years following the 1990s, Sunday school teachings, although similar, were adapted to the reality of computerization as resources for curriculum became widely available from a variety of sources. There were changes in Anglican practices in subsequent years too – children of all ages could participate in Holy Communion, which was previously restricted to those who had received Confirmation. Less emphasis was placed on rote learning in the Sunday school classroom and more thought was given to providing a relevant and meaningful curriculum suitable for children of all ages. The Godly Play program has been used with much success.

The Godly Play approach has been influenced by the philosophy of Maria Montessori and involves children in a multi-sensory way so they can experience the wonder and mystery of God.

Children in the Sunday school program are also presented with their own Bible when they reach Grade 3 in order to encourage Bible reading at home.

Other activities have become popular in recent years also such as Kids Camp or VBS, a week-long morning program offered in the summer months to children in Sunday school and the community. To date we have hosted six summer camps for children who enjoyed a week of fun, games and songs while learning about Jesus. Fall parties were also enjoyed by families over the years, as well as the annual Christmas Pageant when the children presented the story of Jesus' birth to the congregation during the morning service.

Perhaps one of the most notable initiatives over the last few years has been the role of outreach with our younger church members. Sunday school at St. John the Divine is also called K.I.D.S. Club, which means "Kids in Divine Service," and the objective of our program has been to provide a place where children learn about God's great love for them and to demonstrate how to serve others as Jesus taught. Our projects have included raising money to help with PWRDF's "World of Gifts" program, the Sleeping Children Around the World program, the school lunches for Haiti program, the World Wildlife Fund to support efforts to save wildlife as a result of wildfires in Australia, and a book sale to raise funds for Hurricane Dorian relief. Children in Sunday school have been taught that every child has the power to change the world through service to others – it is by training children up in the teachings of Jesus that we instill in them the importance of service as a lifelong activity. Our work continues.

> *"Train up a child in the way he should go; and when he is old he will not depart from it."*

Proverbs 22:6

OTHER GATHERINGS AT ST. JOHN THE DIVINE

Outside of regular worship services, Sunday school, Youth Group, Ladies Friendship Group etc., are the many ways in which the community has come together in a social manner. As we are the country church on the edge of the city, food plays an important role in any social gathering. Candlelit dinners, Shrove Tuesday pancake suppers, BBQs, Harvest Hoedown, spaghetti dinners, Eating Together Group and Culturefest are just a few of the ways we celebrate one another's company. And coffee hour following church is really lunch for the faithful that gather. Each week, a family takes turns making coffee, tea, juice and sweet and savoury delectables. In fact, St. John's has a reputation of having the best coffee hour in the Diocese.

Each year the parish is involved in a Bible Study that occurs on a weekday as well as in Advent and Lenten studies. Parishioners are also welcomed at services outside of Sunday mornings. Ash Wednesday, Maundy Thursday and Good Friday are a few of the services of worship offered. Maundy Thursday involves a potluck dinner followed by worship. Over the past five years, the United Church has joined us (first Arva United and then Siloam United) for dinner and worship. One of the favourite services is our annual Christmas Pageant presented by our Sunday school under the direction of Muriel Vincent.

OUTREACH COMMITTEE
BY: CINDY NICHOLSON

In the fall of 2017, a new committee was formed to serve people both within and beyond our parish. This was in response to a call to live out all aspects of the Five Marks of Mission. They include:

- To proclaim the Good News of the Kingdom
- To teach, baptize and nurture new believers
- To respond to human need by loving service
- To seek to transform unjust structures of society, to challenge violence of every kind and to pursue peace and reconciliation
- To strive to safeguard the integrity of creation and sustain and renew the life of the earth

The Committee has been grateful for the kind and generous support of our congregation for new and continuing outreach projects, a reflection of God's love in action in our community.

PWRDF Donations

During the Christmas season, congregants have given generous donations toward boxes of cards to support the Primate's World Relief and Development Fund. PWRDF is the official development and relief agency of the Anglican Church of Canada. The money raised is used to fund their programs and address issues such as poverty, food security and preventative health both in Canada and around the world. Additional funds have been raised through plant and marmalade sales to support Indigenous maternal health and the development of midwifery training programs.

Help for a Refugee Family

In November 2017, a Congolese refugee family of two adults and six children sustained a terrible fire at their London townhome. A special collection at one service totalled $1280.00 to support the family.

Canadian Foodrains Good Neighbour Project

In 2017, our church joined this project, which is a group of rural and London-based churches who grow crops on a dedicated plot of land to harvest and sell at market value. The proceeds are donated to the Canadian Foodgrains Bank which works to end global hunger and are matched 4:1 by the Canadian government. The Outreach Group at St. John's has been supportive of the project through various activities such as a marmalade sale, attendance at the annual barbeque and through direct donation. Our current representative for the project is Jim Colbert.

Food Drives

Three times a year, food drives are organized by our committee in order to collect non-perishable food items for donation to the Daily Bread Food Bank at St. Paul's Cathedral. An outing to the London and Area Food Bank was also arranged so congregation members could help with the sorting and bagging of food gifts for needy families.

The Angel Tree

The Angel Tree Program has been a favourite outreach initiative at St. John's for quite some time and provides an opportunity for members to be "an angel" to someone during the Christmas season. Gifts have been provided in recent years to children and families in schools and lower-income neighbourhoods in the city, Rotholme Women's and Family Shelter, The Children's Aid Society, Extendicare Nursing Home, and a refugee family and several families serviced by the Northwest London Resource Centre. The Angel Tree Program has become a Christmas tradition at St. John's that is loved and well supported by the congregation.

Old East Village Explosion

Following the devastating explosion on Woodman Avenue in August 2019, parishioners lovingly provided money, gift cards, clothes and toys to support the people affected.

Soktober

In 2019, the Outreach Group launched a new initiative for the month of October requesting socks, the most needed items at homeless shelters. We had a wonderful response from the congregation and were happy to deliver many pairs of socks for men, women and children to Mission Services of London.

Home Visiting Program

To help support Rev. Wendy Mencel's home visiting program, the Youth Group and the Outreach Committee prepared casseroles and baked cookies and squares to ensure that there was an inventory of food gifts to bring on her visits.

Medway High School Pizza Lunch

An exciting outreach to Medway High School students was initiated in February 2019. On the first Thursday of each month in the school year, we have welcomed students for a pizza lunch during their two lunch periods. Our goals are to provide a warm, loving, safe and welcoming Christian environment, and a break from the demands of school. We hope to provide opportunities for students to develop positive relationships and engage in conversation with each other, with Rev. Wendy Mencel, and adult volunteers from our outreach ministry. The program also helps students who may not be comfortable in the busy cafeteria environment and may seek extra encouragement and support in a welcoming church community.

Word has reached our community partners and private donors who have been very interested in supporting this initiative, knowing that mental health and spiritual health have been closely tied together. We are grateful to The Diocesan Golf Tournament Committee, The Order of the Eastern

Star, The Arva Optimists, The Thorndale Optimists, The Thorndale Lions and the Ilderton Lions. All this support has been a huge blessing to this ministry, which has grown steadily. Seventy-five students attended our first lunch, then three hundred, and eventually the lunches averaged over four hundred students per lunch.

With these increasing numbers, Rev. Wendy has welcomed students in both the parish hall and the sanctuary. Students often ask her questions about God, about the church and about religion. It is a beautiful sight!

When the Covid-19 pandemic is managed and students and parishioners are once again able to have time together, we will all look forward to resuming the "Church Lunch."

As of the time of writing this, we are in the midst of the Covid-19 pandemic. From March of 2020 until September of 2020 all worship had to be moved online. This posed a great challenge to Rev. Wendy and was a "baptism by fire" to have her up and running for the new reality. However, we succeeded and have been now recording our live services now that we are back in church. The pandemic has certainly cemented the reality of online worship, and this format will continue in conjunction with in-person worship.

The past two hundred years have seen great change both in society and in church, and we anticipate and welcome the changes to come. We are a Christian people who await the coming again of the Lord all the while working to bring the Kingdom of God to our here and now. Thanks be to God.

www.ingramcontent.com/pod-product-compliance
Lightning Source LLC
LaVergne TN
LVHW021740060526
838200LV00052B/3391